KILLER WHALES

by Charnan Simon and Ariel Kazunas

Children's Press®

An Imprint of Scholastic Inc.
New York Toronto London Auckland Sydney
Mexico City New Delhi Hong Kong
Danbury, Connecticut

Content Consultant
Dr. Stephen S. Ditchkoff
Professor of Wildlife Sciences
Auburn University
Auburn, Alabama

Photographs © 2013: age fotostock: cover, 7 (H Schmidbauer/
Blickwinkel), 8 (Michael S. Nolan); Alamy Images/MIXA: 36;
Bob Italiano: 44 foreground, 45 foreground; Dreamstime: 1, 2
foreground, 3 foreground, 46 (Jami Garrison), 5 top, 11 (Krystof),
2 background, 3 background, 44 background, 45 background
(Natalia Pavlova); Getty Images/Jens Kuhfs: 40; Media Bakery/Don
Paulson: 28; National Geographic Stock/J. Baylor Roberts: 32; Photo
Researchers/Francois Gohier: 16; Shutterstock, Inc.: 27 (Bristock
Studios), 35 (palmenprep); Superstock, Inc.: 5 bottom, 31 (age
fotostock), 4, 5 background, 23, 24 (Gerard Lacz/age fotostock), 12,
15, 19, 20, 39 (Minden Pictures).

Library of Congress Cataloging-in-Publication Data
Simon, Charnan.
   Killer whales/by Charnan Simon and Ariel Kazunas.
      p. cm.–(Nature's children)
   Includes bibliographical references and index.
   ISBN-13: 978-0-531-26834-6 (lib. bdg.)
   ISBN-13: 978-0-531-25479-0 (pbk.)
   1. Killer whale–Juvenile literature. I. Kazunas, Ariel. II. Title.
   QL737.C432S545 2013
   599.53'6–dc23   2012000636

All rights reserved. Published in 2013 by Children's Press, an imprint
of Scholastic Inc.
Printed in China 62
SCHOLASTIC, CHILDREN'S PRESS, and associated logos are
trademarks and/or registered trademarks of Scholastic Inc.

2 3 4 5 6 7 8 9 10 R 22 21 20 19 18 17 16 15 14 13

Killer Whales

Class	Mammalia
Order	Cetacea
Family	Delphinidae
Genus	*Orcinus*
Species	*Orcinus orca*
World distribution	The most widely distributed marine mammals; found in all oceans, from the Arctic to the Antarctic; most common in colder waters
Habitat	Ocean
Distinctive physical characteristics	Black on top with white undersides and white patches near their eyes and behind their dorsal fins; average males are between 19 and 22 feet (5.8 and 6.7 meters) long and weigh about 10,000 pounds (4,536 kilograms); average females are between 16 and 19 feet (4.9 and 5.8 m) long and weigh about 5,500 pounds (2,495 kg)
Habits	Highly social animals; live together in family groups called pods; hunt cooperatively to capture prey; make a wide variety of communicative sounds
Diet	Fish, squid, sharks, penguins, seals, sea lions, porpoises, and other marine mammals, depending upon location

Contents

Meet the Killer Whale

Killer whales, or orcas, are huge **predators**. With their wide mouths and sharp teeth, they have been known to eat everything from small fish to whales more than twice their size. This is where their name comes from. Because of their size and power, people once feared killer whales.

Yet these fierce hunters are much more than mindless killers. They are highly intelligent, curious, and playful. Their social groups are very complex. They play together, communicate with each other, and help each other hunt. Despite their size, they can be both quick and agile. Their intelligence and grace have also made them a favorite at **marine** parks and on boat tours. There they leap high out of the water and sometimes splash the people watching them. Their looks also make them hard to forget. The distinctive black and white markings make this whale easy to recognize!

A killer whale leaping from the water is an incredible sight.

Huge Dolphins

Killer whales are the largest members of the dolphin family. The average male weighs about 10,000 pounds (4,536 kilograms) and is between 19 and 22 feet (5.8 and 6.7 meters) long. That is more than twice the size of most other dolphins!

Like all dolphins, killer whales are **mammals**, not fish. They have lungs and breathe air, just like mammals that live on land. A killer whale breathes through a blowhole on top of its head. When the whale dives underwater, its blowhole shuts tightly. When it surfaces, it blows out the air and takes another breath. Some killer whales can hold their breath for more than 15 minutes at a time.

Adult Male
6 ft. (1.8 m)

20 ft. (6.1 meters)

Killer whales shoot clouds of mist into the air when they breathe out through their blowholes.

CHAPTER 2

Powerful Predators

Killer whales have muscular, streamlined bodies that are built for speed. Killer whales use their powerful flukes to push themselves through the water. They use their flippers to help steer and turn. Dorsal fins on the tops of their bodies help keep them steady. Orcas can swim as fast as 30 miles (48 kilometers) per hour. They can travel as far as 100 miles (161 km) in a single day. Because they are so fast and strong, killer whales have few enemies in the ocean.

In addition to keeping them safe from other animals, killer whales' bodies protect them from their environment. Many killer whales live in very cold water. They have thick layers of fat called blubber to keep them warm. Their circulatory system protects them from the cold by moving warm blood through their bodies.

Killer whales use their fins and flippers to make fast turns and twists as they move through the water.

Fierce Hunters

A killer whale's huge jaws are lined with as many as 56 sharp teeth. Some of these teeth can be as long as 4 inches (10 centimeters). When the orca catches prey, its jaws snap tightly together. Even large animals such as walruses find it hard to escape from this trap.

Killer whales don't need to chew their food. Their throats are big enough to swallow most prey whole. They tear larger prey into chunks before swallowing it.

A killer whale's black-and-white coloring acts as camouflage to help the orca sneak up on prey. A seal lying on an ice floe might not see a killer whale swimming beneath it because the whale's black back blends into the dark water. Fish swimming below the killer whale might not see it because its white belly blends in with the light coming from above the water's surface.

Orcas use their sharp teeth to get a grip on prey.

A Sixth Sense

Killer whales have very good eyesight. They can spot prey both underwater and above the surface. But even with such good vision, killer whales can only see so far underwater. They have an especially hard time seeing at night. Instead of using their eyes, they often rely on a remarkable sense known as echolocation.

As a killer whale swims through the ocean, it makes fast, high-pitched clicking sounds. These clicks travel through the water as sound waves. The sound waves bounce off objects in the water and come back to the orca as echoes. The orca's brain uses these echoes to "see" its surroundings.

Killer whales use echolocation to learn the size, shape, speed, distance, and direction of objects in the water. They can also use it to send out powerful sound waves that hit some smaller prey hard enough to stun or kill it!

Echolocation helps killer whales find prey even when
cloudy water makes it difficult for them to see.

Wolves of the Sea

Killer whales are sometimes called the wolves of the sea. Like wolf packs, orca pods use teamwork to capture their prey. Very few ocean animals can defend themselves against a pod of hungry killer whales.

Sometimes killer whales circle groups of small fish, such as herring. They swim around and around, forcing the fish into a cluster near the surface. They then use their tails to slap the fish. This stuns them and makes them easy to catch.

Orcas use other methods to attack larger prey such as sharks or whales. They often surround the prey to keep it from escaping. Then some of the killer whales ram the prey with their heads or slap it with their tails. Others leap onto the prey's back, biting and tearing with their sharp teeth.

Killer whales work together to take down large prey such as other whales.

More Ways to Hunt

Some killer whales hunt marine mammals and birds. Sometimes they use their heads to bump penguins and sea lions off ice floes. Other times, they use their tails to push waves over the floes. This washes prey into the water, where the orcas can easily catch it. Eyewitnesses in Alaska once saw two orcas flip an ice floe onto its side to slide a sleeping seal right into the mouth of a third orca!

Sometimes killer whales slide right up on the shore to catch prey. They grab seals or sea lions from beaches and drag them into the water. It takes skill to crash through the surf and catch a seal. The orca must be careful not to get stuck on the beach. Beached whales die if they cannot get back into the ocean.

FUN FACT! Killer whales have been discovered with the remains of other killer whales in their stomachs.

Orcas can snatch prey such as sea lions from the shores of beaches.

CHAPTER 3

The Wonders of Whales

Killer whales are very social animals. Most live in family groups called pods. Pods can have as few as two or as many as 100 members. Members of the pod hunt together, feed together, and play together.

The leader of a pod is usually the oldest female. The pod is built around this female and her **offspring**. Orca family bonds are very strong. Offspring often stay with their mothers even after they are fully grown. It isn't unusual for an orca pod to contain four **generations** of related whales.

Killer whales live a long time in the wild. Males usually live for about 30 years, but some live as long as 50 or 60 years. Females usually live to be about 50 years old, but some have been known to live for more than 80 years. These older females have a lot of experience surviving in the ocean. They pass along their knowledge to the rest of the pod.

Pod members can range widely in age.

21

Growing Up in the Pod

Female orcas give birth to one **calf** at a time. A newborn orca calf weighs around 400 pounds (181 kg) and is about 8 feet (2.4 m) long.

Orca calves are usually born tail first. As soon as a newborn calf slips into the water, its mother pushes it to the surface so it can breathe. Then the calf starts to drink its mother's rich, creamy milk. This milk helps the calf build up a thick layer of blubber so it can stay warm in the cold water.

The calf continues to drink its mother's milk for up to two years. During this time, it rarely leaves its mother's side. As the calf grows, other members of the pod teach it hunting and swimming skills and play with it. An orca pod is a big group of sisters, brothers, cousins, aunts, uncles, and grandparents. These family members all take care of each other.

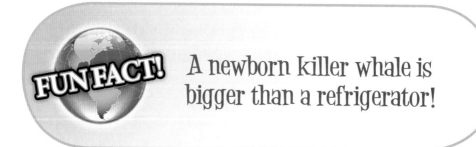

FUN FACT! A newborn killer whale is bigger than a refrigerator!

Young orcas stay close to their mothers.

Communication Is Everything

Killer whales communicate with each other using a variety of sounds, including clicks, whistles, and squeaks. Each pod has its own special set of sounds. The orcas can recognize their family members calling from miles away.

An orca calf must be taught how to communicate with the other members of its pod. The calf listens to its mother and imitates the sounds she makes. Soon it can make the same noises as adult orcas.

Killer whales also communicate with orcas outside of their own pods. Some pods are related to other pods, much like humans have cousins and other extended family members. These related pods sometimes hunt or travel together. They communicate using similar sounds. This means killer whales that live in related pods can understand each other.

Killer whales also communicate using body language. Mothers and calves nuzzle each other often. Adults rub and roll against each other as they swim. Touching in this way helps pod members stay closely connected to one another.

Killer whales nuzzle each other to show affection.

A Killer Whale's Day

Killer whales spend much of their time foraging. Foraging is when they actively eat or hunt for food. They spend less time foraging when there is a lot of food available. They spend more time foraging when food is scarce. Killer whales share what they catch with fellow pod members and don't fight over food. An average adult orca eats about 500 pounds (227 kg) of food a day.

Killer whales also spend a great deal of time traveling from one part of the ocean to another. Traveling orcas swim quickly and steadily, without stopping. They are usually moving from one feeding ground to another. Pod members often come up to the surface and dive together all at once.

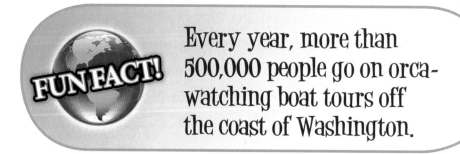

FUN FACT! Every year, more than 500,000 people go on orca-watching boat tours off the coast of Washington.

It is common to see killer whales surfacing in large groups.

Three Kinds of Killer Whales

Most killer whales studied in the wild come from the northern part of the Pacific Ocean. Researchers have observed these whales' social habits and movements and have organized them into three categories.

Resident orcas rarely move from their home areas near coastlines. This makes them easier to observe. There are usually between five and 50 whales in a resident pod. Most of what scientists know about killer whales comes from studying the resident pods that live in the protected coastal waters of the Pacific Northwest.

Transient orcas travel up and down the Pacific Coast from southern California to Alaska. They stay close to the shoreline, where they can find marine mammals such as seals and porpoises to eat. They usually live alone or in small groups of between two and six whales.

Offshore orcas usually live in very large pods of 30 to 60 whales. They like to swim in the open sea. Because offshore orcas rarely come close to shore, scientists don't know much about them.

Scientists follow killer whale pods as they move through the ocean.

Light Sleepers

Like all animals, killer whales need to sleep sometimes. But orcas don't sleep soundly the way people do. If they fell completely asleep while underwater, they would drown. Scientists think that orcas sleep by resting their brains one half at a time. While one half sleeps, the other half stays awake to control swimming and breathing.

Killer whales swim very slowly while they are sleeping. The whole pod clusters close together. The orcas sleep, breathe, and move at the same time. They stay very quiet. One or two orcas may stay awake at the edge of the pod. They act as lookouts in case of danger.

After sleeping, killer whales are often ready to socialize. They breach by leaping out of the water, do belly flops, and slap their flukes on the surface of the water. They squeak, grunt, and whistle at each other. These behaviors may help the whales practice important survival skills.

A breaching orca is an amazing sight.

CHAPTER 4

Out of the Past

Whales have lived on Earth for a long time. But their ancestors looked very different from today's orcas. Many scientists believe that early whale ancestors lived mostly on land, not water. As these whale ancestors began spending more time in the water, their bodies changed. Over time, they grew strong tails to propel them along. They lost the back legs they no longer needed. Their front arms became wide flippers, perfect for swimming.

Scientists learn about these ancient animals by studying fossils. The earliest types of whale fossils discovered so far are about 50 million years old. But killer whales like the ones that live today probably didn't exist that long ago. The earliest killer whale fossils are between 2.6 million and 5.3 million years old.

FUN FACT! An X-ray of an orca flipper shows hand-like and finger-like bones.

Paleontologists study a whale vertebra found in sandy cliffs by a bay.

Dolphin Cousins

Killer whales belong to the dolphin family. All dolphins are a type of whale known as a cetacean, or toothed whale. The earliest dolphins probably appeared on Earth about 11 million years ago. Today, there are about 36 different species of dolphins living throughout the world's oceans and rivers.

Dolphins range widely in size and shape. The smallest species is the Hector's dolphin. It grows to weigh about 110 pounds (50 kg). An average Hector's dolphin is about 4 feet (1.2 m) long. Almost all dolphin species are fast swimmers, and they are usually friendly to humans.

The most famous type of dolphin is the bottlenose. These playful, intelligent animals often perform amazing tricks in shows at aquariums and zoos. Some have even starred in movies and television shows. However, more and more people are realizing that these animals belong in the ocean, not in captivity.

Bottlenose dolphins are beloved for their friendly, playful nature.

CHAPTER 5

Into the Future

Killer whales have lived in Earth's oceans for millions of years, but their future is uncertain. Because of the actions of humans, orcas are endangered in some parts of the world.

Throughout history, many people feared and hated orcas. They knew orcas were fierce killers. They were afraid orcas might attack and kill people, too. Not everyone felt this way, though. First Nation peoples along the West Coast of North America respected the orcas' strength and beauty. They celebrated orcas in art, songs, and stories.

Humans have long caused trouble for orcas. Hunting is one major problem. For many years, people have killed all kinds of whales for the oils and fats in their bodies. Killer whales have not been hunted as much as other whales. They're harder to catch, and they don't have as much oil and blubber as other whales do. Still, hunters have killed thousands of orcas over the years.

If fishermen overfish, it leaves less food for orcas and other marine predators.

Trouble Ahead

In some places, orcas are running out of food. Many orcas rely on salmon to survive. But several species of salmon are also endangered because of overfishing and **habitat** loss. Without enough salmon, many orcas will starve to death.

Humans have also **polluted** the oceans with oil spills, trash, and other harmful substances. Polluted water is very unhealthy for killer whales. Calves are especially likely to get sick if they swim in contaminated water.

Boats are also a threat to killer whales. Orcas can get hurt if they collide with boats. They can get trapped in nets from fishing boats. Worst of all, the noise from boat engines makes it hard for them to use echolocation. Without echolocation, killer whales can't find their way through the ocean. They can't find food or communicate with their pods. After getting lost and swimming in the wrong direction, some whales even get stuck on the shores of beaches.

The left whale's fin was likely damaged by a boat or other fishing equipment.

Orcas Survive

...ere often caught and put into
...s gave people their first chance
...rned more about them, many
... to take wild orcas away from
... to capture killer whales in U.S.
...an 50 orcas in captivity. Scientists
... habitat. Every day, they learn
...t, and communicate.
...help killer whales survive. We can
...ceans and build healthy populations
...can try to keep boats away from
...we can learn to share our oceans
...with killer whales.

Whales sometimes poke their heads above water to examine their suroundings.
This is called spyhopping.

Words to Know

ancestors (AN-ses-turz) — ancient animal species that are related to modern species

breach (BREECH) — launch above the surface of the water

calf (KAF) — the young of several large species of animals, such as dolphins, cows, and seals

camouflage (KAM-o-flaj) — coloring or body shape that allows an animal to blend in with its surroundings

captivity (kap-TIV-i-tee) — the condition of being held or trapped by people

circulatory system (SIR-kyeh-leh-tor-ee SIS-tuhm) — the group of organs that pump blood through the body

dorsal fins (DOR-suhl FINZ) — tall, triangular fins found on the backs of whales

echolocation (eh-koh-loh-KAY-shuhn) — process of using sound waves to locate the position of objects in the water

endangered (en-DAYN-jurd) — at risk of becoming extinct, usually because of human activity

flukes (FLOOKS) — tail fins of a sea creature, such as a whale or dolphin

foraging (FOR-ij-ing) — searching for food

fossils (FOSS-uhlz) — the hardened remains of prehistoric plants and animals

generations (jen-uh-RAY-shunz) — animals or individuals born around the same time

habitat (HAB-uh-tat) — the place where an animal or a plant is usually found ice floe (ISE FLOH) — a large sheet or block of floating ice in a sea, lake, or river

mammals (MAM-uhlz) — warm-blooded animals that have hair or fur and usually give birth to live young

marine (muh-REEN) — any animal, place, or thing that is related to the sea

offspring (AWF-spring) — the young of an animal or a human being

pods (PAHDZ) — groups of certain kinds of sea animals, such as dolphins and other whales

polluted (puh-LOO-tid) — contaminated by harmful materials that damage the air, water, and soil

predators (PREH-duh-turz) — animals that live by hunting other animals for food

prey (PRAY) — an animal that's hunted by another animal for food

species (SPEE-sheez) — one of the groups into which animals and plants of the same genus are divided

PACIFIC

OCEAN

NORTH

AMERICA

ATLANTIC

SOUTH
AMERICA

Killer Whale Range

ARCTIC OCEAN

EUROPE

ASIA

AFRICA

INDIAN
OCEAN

OCEAN

PACIFI
OCEAN

AUSTRALIA

Find Out More

Books

Armour, Michael. *Orca Song*. Norwalk, CT: Soundprints/Smithsonian Oceanic Collection, 2011.

Arnold, Caroline. *A Killer Whale's World*. Minneapolis: Picture Window Books, 2006.

Gish, Melissa. *Killer Whales*. Mankato, MN: Creative Paperbacks, 2011.

Markle, Sandra. *Killer Whales: Animal Predators*. Minneapolis: Carolrhoda Books, 2004.

Visit this Scholastic Web site for more information on killer whales:
www.factsfornow.scholastic.com
Enter the keyword **Killer whales**

Index

About the Authors

Charnan Simon is a former editor of *Cricket* magazine and has written more than 100 books for young readers. She is lucky to have seen killer whales up close and personal in the Salish Sea of Washington State and British Columbia.

Ariel Kazunas is a writer, artist, and outdoor adventurer who has written a number of books for young readers. She learned much of what she knows about killer whales from her sister Hana, marine biologist and orca expert extraordinaire.